GRAND TETON
NATIONAL PARK

A VISUAL INTERPRETATION

Essay
by
Jackie Gilmore

SIERRA PRESS, INC.

GRAND TETON
NATIONAL PARK

A VISUAL
INTERPRETATION

Essay
by
Jackie Gilmore

Mount Moran and Jackson Lake from Colter Bay, summer evening.

Glacier below North Face of the Grand Teton.

Horses grazing below storm-shrouded Tetons, late spring.

FRONT COVER PHOTO: Aspens and the Grand Teton seen from near Oxbow Bend.
BACK COVER PHOTO: The Teton Range from Snake River Overlook, winter dawn.

ISBN O-939365-44-8

Copyright 1995 by The Sierra Press, Inc.

Printed in Singapore.
First Edition: Spring 1995.

ACKNOWLEDGEMENTS

We would like to take this opportunity to thank the many photographers who made their imagery available to us during the editing of this title. While no single image can effectively replace the actual experience of being there, we believe the visual story told by the images contained in this volume do tell the story of seasonal change and process more effectively than what the visitor would experience while on vacation.
We would also like to thank Sharlene Milligan and her staff at Grand Teton Natural History Association, as well as the Interpretive Staff at Grand Teton National Park, whose assistance has helped in the creation and formation of this book— Thank You!

DEDICATION

This book is a visual tribute to the insight of those few who saw the wisdom of setting aside such a tract of land for the future, without regard for personal gain. That the National Park Service and its components have become a model for more than 130 countries from around the world is all the proof that is necessary to confirm their wisdom. We can only hope our own use is consistent with this wisdom and in no way contributes to the degradation of this most extraordinary legacy.
In this spirit, let us all pledge to continue to work, and sacrifice, for the greater good of places such as Grand Teton National Park.

SIERRA PRESS, INC.

4988 Gold Leaf Drive, Mariposa, CA 95338

CONTENTS

GRAND TETON
NATIONAL PARK

ESSAY
by
JACKIE GILMORE

The Tetons reflected in a beaver pond.

G rand Teton National Park, in northwestern Wyoming, is a land of incredible diversity and beauty. The rugged peaks of the Teton Range dominate the valley of Jackson Hole. The interplay of light and weather changes the colors and moods of the Tetons from day to day, season to season. Alpine meadows, sheer rock faces, glacier-carved canyons, and mountain streams greet the high-altitude hiker. River bottoms, lakes, meadows, and sagebrush-grasslands are found in the valley below. Mountains and water, wildflowers and trees, mammals and birds, temperate summers and frigid winters contribute to the character of this mountain landscape.

This 310,000-acre national park is part of the Greater Yellowstone Ecosystem, an area encompassing approximately 28,000 contiguous square miles in Wyoming, Montana, and Idaho. The Greater Yellowstone region is not defined by political boundaries but rather by the relationships among the topography, geology, hydrology, geothermal features, climate, plants, and wildlife that are found in this vast area. It includes Yellowstone and Grand Teton national parks, the National Elk Refuge, Red Rock Lakes and Gray's Lake national wildlife refuges, and seven national forests.

The Teton Range runs north and south, and the east side rises abruptly above the valley of Jackson Hole. Spruce, fir, pine, and aspen forests blend with rocks on the lower slopes of the mountainside, but above treeline, at about 10,000 feet, the massive rocks have hard edges and angles that are indicative of geologically young mountains. As the Tetons age over more millions of years, the jagged rocks and steep slopes will be worn down by weather and erosion.

Arrowleaf balsamroot and the Teton Range, early summer.

MOUNTAIN BUILDING

It is easy to contemplate the immensity of the earth when you stand in the valley and look up to the summit of the Grand Teton, 13,770 feet above sea level and more than a mile above your head. It is more difficult to comprehend the time it took the forces of nature to create such a magnificent scene.

More than 2.5 billion years ago, volcanic debris and sand settled on the bottom of an ancient ocean. For millions of years, this buried sediment was changed, or metamorphosed, by heat and pressure—creating gneiss. Granite was created, when magma pushed through weak spots in the gneiss and cooled. Gneiss makes up the main rock mass of the Teton range, and the central peaks are granite.

From 80 million to 40 million years ago, the continent's crust was compressed—resulting in the uplift of the Rocky Mountain chain, running north and south from Canada to Mexico. However, the Teton Range, part of the Rockies, did not begin to rise until about 9 million years ago. The Teton fault was created as a result of stretching and thinning of the earth's crust. The block to the west of the fault thrust upwards, as if on a hinge, to form the mountains, and the block to the east of the fault dropped and eventually became the valley. The mountain block has been uplifted only about one fourth as much as the valley block has dropped. This movement along the fault has produced

scarps more than thirty four miles long and up to fifty meters high, some of which are visible along the base of the mountains.

Recent research indicates that the latest fault displacements of thirteen to fourteen feet were caused by two earthquakes and included one slip of roughly nine feet about 7,175 years ago and a second slip of approximately four feet more recently—this date is still unknown. Although evidence indicates that the Teton fault has been seismically quiet in historic time, geologists estimate that it has the potential to produce an earthquake with a magnitude of 6.9–7.5 at any time in the future.

Displacement on the Teton fault has been almost 30,000 vertical feet, but today we can only see a difference in elevation between the mountain summits and the valley floor of about 7,000 feet. Volcanic flows from Yellowstone, rock debris carried by glaciers, and rocks and sediments from erosion have filled in much of the valley.

Following the mountain uplift, glaciers moved through the region sculpting and scouring the earth. A massive glacier, 2,000 feet thick in some places, flowed south through the valley about 150,000 years ago. It stopped just north of the present town of Jackson and melted. About 60,000 years ago, glaciers returned and moved from the east through the Buffalo River valley, then turned south into Jackson Hole. The most recent glacial period, about 20,000 years

A young bison calf.

ago, saw ice advance from the Yellowstone Plateau down the Snake River drainage, while other glaciers moved down the Teton mountains to the valley floor.

As the glaciers moved down the mountainsides, they widened the V-shaped canyons that had been cut by streams and created the familiar U-shaped canyons that indicate the passage of ice. On reaching the valley floor, they gouged deep holes in the earth, melted, then deposited piles of rock debris called moraines, which acted as dams for the glacial meltwaters. Leigh, String, Jenny, Bradley, Taggart, and Phelps lakes, located at or near the base of the mountains, were created during this last glacial period. The moraines around the lakes contain silt and clay, which support growth of lodgepole pine and subalpine fir. Today, twelve reestablished glaciers exist, and some of these can be seen from the valley floor.

WEATHER AND WILDLIFE

Weather is a dominant force in the Tetons, affecting all living and nonliving things. Frost, snow, wind, and water add definition to the always-changing landscape. Warm temperatures and blue skies are the daily fare in summer months, although a snowstorm can materialize in the high mountains at any time. Brief thunderstorms add drama to late summer afternoons, and rainbows delight the eye. In early summer wildflowers burst into bright colors, and aspen and cottonwoods are green and full.

The gentle days of summer nurture the newborns of the year. Elk, deer, bison, and moose tend their young in meadows, forests, and wetlands. Eagles and hawks, swans and ducks, songbirds and hummingbirds are busy quelling the voracious appetites of their nestlings. A small population of black bears can often be found in mountain canyons and the forests along the base of the mountains. More frequent sightings of grizzly bears indicate that they may be moving from Yellowstone into the Tetons.

Badgers and coyotes prowl the meadows and grasslands hunting for mice, voles, and ground squirrels. Red squirrels, chipmunks, and golden-mantled ground squirrels are common in and near forested areas, while river otters, muskrats, and mink live along streams, ponds, and lakes.

The high elevation and northern latitude of the Tetons bring an early autumn. Frosty nights and warm days of September add new color to the valley and mountainsides as deciduous trees and shrubs turn from green to yellow, gold, and red. The skies seem bluer in the crisp autumn air, and the calm days belie what's to come. Wildlife activity intensifies as birds and animals prepare for the oncoming winter. Canada geese fly

Historic barn at the Moulton Ranch.

above the valley gaining strength for a southerly migration flight. Hummingbirds and many songbirds have departed. Juvenile trumpeter swans are in their final growth stage and soon will be ready to follow the adults to their wintering grounds.

Uinta ground squirrels have disappeared, already hibernating in tunnels underneath the grassy meadows where they spent a brief summer feeding and raising young. Beavers swim back and forth from stands of willows, aspen, and cottonwoods collecting branches for a winter food supply. They anchor them firmly underwater near the entrance to their lodges, then go back for more.

Pikas collect and dry plants for "haypiles" found under large boulders in talus slopes and rock slides where they will spend winter, and yellow-bellied marmots are hibernating in burrows below the rocks. Elk, moose, pronghorns, and deer are occupied with courtship and mating rituals and will migrate to wintering areas as the weather continues to cool.

Wildlife abundance and activity is affected by the weather; to be successful in this ecosystem, it is necessary to adjust to the winters either by being adaptive to cold weather, by hibernating, or by migrating to a more temperate location. Pronghorns (antelope) travel to southern Wyoming to winter, while other ungulates stay in the valley, moving to places where food is most accessible. The National Elk Refuge, north of the town of Jackson and contiguous to park lands, provides winter range for more than 7,000 elk.

The blustery days of November bring winter weather to the Tetons, and by December, the landscape is white from the top of the mountains to the valley floor. Nothing escapes the snow, as it blows and drifts into every crack and crevice. The snow depth on the valley floor ranges from one to four feet and the mountain snow pack can exceed one hundred inches. Winter temperatures reflect the northern latitude and high elevations. During the coldest days of winter the temperature can drop to minus forty degrees Fahrenheit at night, with daytime highs well below zero. The weather moderates as spring approaches, but temperatures are usually below freezing both day and night. Some of the snow may melt during a brief period of warmer weather, but rarely does the ground appear until spring. The land is locked in winter for about five months.

At the spring equinox, the park is still in winter, but warming winds and longer days begin to melt away the persistent snow. By April, the valley is melted free and the mountain snow pack is shrinking. Creeks and rivers swell with runoff, sage buttercups and spring beauties bloom on open ground, and migrant birds and mammals begin to arrive. The future holds the promise of wildflowers and warm days as another winter passes.

HUMAN HISTORY

The climate and topography were significant factors in the human use and settlement of this area. Travel to and from the valley in winter was nearly impossible for a person on foot. Deep snow demands snowshoes or skis, and frigid temperatures put humans at risk.

There is archaeological evidence that paleo-Indians came to the valley to hunt game and gather food plants, but they only spent summers here. The discovery of an 8,000-year-old obsidian knife and quartzite projectile point indicate such activities. The Gros Ventres, Flatheads, and other Native American Indian tribes passed through the valley, but the hundreds of archaeological sites have yielded no evidence that the valley was inhabited year-round by any native people.

The first white man to cross Jackson Hole was probably John Colter. He had been part of the Lewis and Clark Expedition for two years and was on his own when he explored the valley in 1807–1808. Following Colter's lead, fur trappers such as Jedediah Smith, William Sublette, and Kit Carson worked in the area. As the trappers roamed the Rockies in search of beavers, they explored and named

many areas. They called valleys that were bordered by mountains "holes" and often named them for a fellow trapper. David Jackson spent considerable time in the Tetons, and the area became known as Jackson's Hole. It is now called Jackson Hole, presumably for simplicity.

Jim Bridger guided the Raynolds expedition through the valley in 1860, and the 1872 Hayden Expedition explored the Tetons and named many features. On the west side of the Teton Range, the Grand, Middle, and South Tetons stand apart from surrounding peaks. French trappers, viewing the mountains from that side, called these three peaks "les trois tetons," or the three breasts, and the name endured.

Finally, in 1884, the first permanent settlers, John Holland and John and Millie Carnes, homesteaded land just north of the present town of Jackson. The population grew slowly as others arrived, but it was only the hardy and most persistent folks that stayed. Small communities sprang up on all sides of the valley, and residents went to great lengths to stay in touch. Social occasions were well attended, and people would travel miles for a dance. In winter, families loaded into their covered sleighs equipped with small wood stoves and drove all day to reach the parties.

Cattle ranching was a significant activity in the valley, and as the

Bull moose, late-summer.

population grew, small businesses were established to provide needed goods and services. Yellowstone National Park had been established in 1872, and wealthy Easterners began to tour the West by train and stagecoach. In the early 1900s, guiding hunters and dude ranching became popular and viable businesses for Jackson Hole residents.

In 1923, five local citizens became concerned over the tourist-oriented development at the base of the Tetons and a private group's attempt to dam Leigh and Jenny lakes for the purpose of selling water to Idaho farmers. Nationally known writer and local dude rancher Struthers Burt was originally against any federal interference in the area, but these developments changed his mind. "I am afraid for my own country," he wrote, "unless some help is given it—some wise direction. It is too beautiful and too famous. Sometimes I dream of it unhappily."

In July, Burt and four others met with Yellowstone National Park Superintendent Horace Albright and proposed that federal protection be given to the Tetons. After heated controversy and debate in the Hole and in Washington, a fledgling Grand Teton National Park was established in 1929. The boundaries included the mountain range and the lakes at the foot of the mountains including Jackson, Jenny, Leigh, String, Bradley, Taggart, and Phelps.

In 1926, when Albright hosted millionaire John D. Rockefeller, Jr. in

Yellowstone, he took Rockefeller on a side trip to the Tetons to share his vision of protecting the area. Rockefeller was both impressed by the beauty of the Tetons and concerned by the already growing tourist development in some of the area's most pristine places. He later decided to purchase lands along the Snake River and in the valley and donate them to the government for additional park lands. These acquisitions were made under the auspices of the Snake River Land Company, purportedly to keep sellers from inflating the prices, and no one realized who was behind the purchases.

When word got out, there was outright hostility and anger toward Rockefeller. Although Rockefeller had paid fair prices for the land, many ranchers did not like the idea of having the land locked up in the federal system. Not only was it grazing and hunting land but the concept of federal ownership was contradictory to their philosophy of individual rights. Controversy once again reigned in the Hole and in Washington, this time over accepting the donated lands and enlarging the park, and no consensus could be reached. Complicated political maneuvers continued until 1950, when Congress finally passed a bill to enlarge the park to include the Snake River and the valley.

EXPLORING THE PARK
More than three million visitors come to Grand Teton annually, and

Bald eagle in cottonwood tree, mid-winter.

summer is by far the most popular time of year. Five campgrounds provide a variety of locations for tent or car camping, while many tourists choose to stay in the lodging available in the park or in the town of Jackson, twelve miles south of the park headquarters. Backcountry campsites are available on a reservation basis.

While spectacular views can be had from the main roads through the park, there are many ac-

tivities to give visitors the opportunity for more personal connections with the land and wildlife. Those with limited time can experience mountain lakes, waterfalls, and grand vistas, while long, steep trails take the hiker high into the alpine zone. Mountain climbers consider the park to have some of the best and most challenging climbing in the country.

The Snake River flows through the park, and rafting, kayaking, and canoeing are popular activities. Motor boats are permitted on the seventeen-mile-long Jackson Lake, and boats with limited horsepower may be used on Jenny Lake. Hand-propelled crafts are allowed on some small lakes, while boating is prohibited on others.

The clean, cold waters of lakes, rivers, and streams provide good fishing. A prize catch is the Snake River cutthroat, the only sport fish native to park waters. It is distinguished by orange-red or red slashes under the cheeks or gills and many small dark spots along both sides. Introduced species include brook, brown, rainbow, and lake trout and Rocky Mountain whitefish.

In winter, cross-country skiers have unlimited choices of terrain and levels of difficulty. Although no trails are groomed specifically for skiing, the most popular treks are packed by skiers. The Teton Park Road in the interior of the park is closed to automobile use and opened to on-road snowmobiling and cross-country skiing. Winter visitor services are very limited although overnight camping is available in the Colter Bay Visitor Center parking lot.

Topography, weather, wildlife, and plants contribute to the ever-changing drama of the Tetons. Whether you hike in alpine meadows, float the Snake River, or ski among snow-laden evergreens, you experience nature from an intimate point of view. In these mountains, the human spirit meets the spirit of the earth.

The historic Cunningham Cabin.

A VISUAL
INTERPRETATION WINTER

The view from Snake River Overlook, winter dawn.

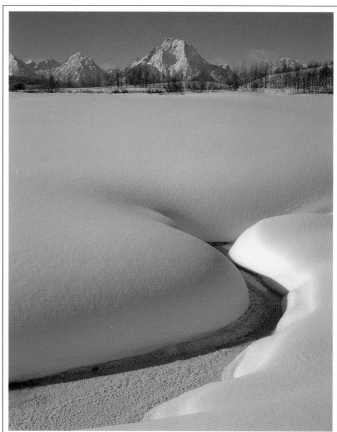

The Grand Teton emerging from winter storm clouds.

Mount Moran seen from Oxbow Bend, mid-winter morning.

Willows and ice, mid-winter.

Patriarch Tree and the Cathedral Group.

The Tetons and split-rail fence, winter morning.

Frosted cottonwood trees, early morning.

Frosted trees along the Snake River.   20

Bison and the Teton Range, winter morning.

A VISUAL INTERPRETATION SPRING & SUMMER

Historic barn near Blacktail Butte, mid-summer.

Sunrise at Jenny Lake, mid-summer.

Pronghorn (antelope).

Wildflower garden of monkeyflower and Indian paintbrush.   24

Yellow fritillary emerging from beneath snow, early spring.

The Tetons seen from South Fork of Cascade Creek, evening.

Mt. Moran and bull moose at Oxbow Bend, dawn.

The Tetons seen from Schwabacher's Landing.

Dandelions, split-rail fence, and the Grand Teton, summer.

Sunset over the Tetons reflected in Jackson Lake.   30

Great gray owl.

Silvery lupine and sagebrush, Antelope Flats.

The Grand Teton seen from Cascade Canyon near Lake Solitude.   32

Morning fog, Snake River Overlook.

Field of fireweed, mid-summer.

Lousewort blooming along the Teton Crest Trail.

A VISUAL
INTERPRETATION AUTUMN

The Grand Teton framed by aspens.

Mt. Moran and Canada geese at Oxbow Bend of the Snake River.   Aspen trunks and leaves, autumn colors.

The Grand Teton and aspens seen from near Oxbow Bend.   38

Cascade mountain ash, autumn color.

Cottonwoods and the Teton Range from near the Gros Ventre River.   40

The Tetons and beaver pond near Schwabacher's Landing.

The Tetons seen from Snake River Overlook, autumn.   42

43　　　　The Grand Teton and Snake River in thick fog, dawn.

A VISUAL INTERPRETATION WINTER: A BRIEF RETURN

The Tetons, winter sunset.

GRAND TETON NATIONAL PARK

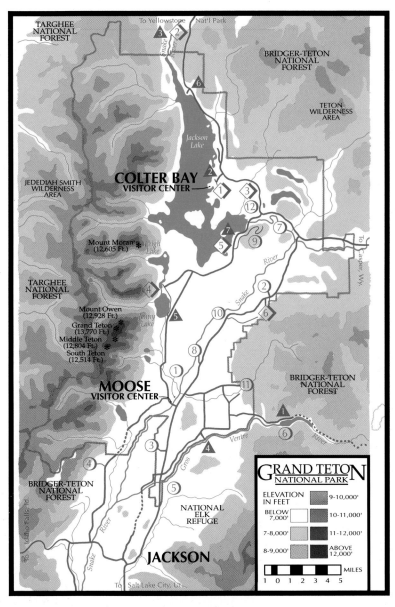

VISITOR CENTERS
- Colter Bay
- Moose (Park Headquarters)

POINTS OF INTEREST
1. Chapel of the Transfiguration & Menor's Ferry
2. Cunningham Cabin
3. Jackson Hole Airport
4. Jackson Hole Ski Area & Teton Village
5. Jackson National Fish Hatchery
6. Lower Slide Lake
7. Oxbow Bend of the Snake River
8. Schwabacher Landing (Raft Launch)
9. Signal Mountain
10. Snake River Overlook
11. Teton Science School
12. Willow Flats

CAMPGROUNDS
1. Atherton Creek (Nat'l Forest)
2. Colter Bay
3. Flagg Ranch (Private)
4. Gros Ventre
5. Jenny Lake (Tents only)
6. Lizard Creek
7. Signal Mountain

LODGING/ACCOMMODATIONS
1. Colter Bay Village
2. Flagg Ranch
3. Jackson Lake Lodge
4. Jenny Lake Lodge
5. Signal Mountain Lodge
6. Triangle X Ranch

Lodging available in the town of Jackson also.